W9-CRM-506

THE SECRET SOCIETY OF MONSTER HUNTERS

The Fairy and the Broken Enchantment

by Leah Kaminski

illustrated by Jared Sams

TORCH GRAPHIC PRESS

Published in the United States of America by Cherry Lake Publishing Group
Ann Arbor, Michigan
www.cherrylakepublishing.com

Reading Adviser: Marla Conn, MS, Ed., Literacy specialist, Read-Ability, Inc.

Photo Credits: page 1: ©djvstock / Getty Images; page 7: ©ArtsyBee / Pixabay; page 7: ©Maudkch / Pixabay; page 9: ©6563351 / Pixabay; page 9: ©ArtsyBee / Pixabay; page 13: ©Clker-Free-Vector-Images / Pixabay; page 29: ©Morozova Olga / shutterstock.com; page (background): ©Mangata / Getty Images

Torch Graphic Press is an imprint of Cherry Lake Publishing Group.

Library of Congress Cataloging-in-Publication Data
Names: Kaminski, Leah, author. | Sams, Jared, illustrator.
Title: The fairy and the broken enchantment / by Leah Kaminski ; illustrated by Jared Sams.
Description: Ann Arbor, Michigan: Torch Graphic Press, 2020. | Series: The Secret Society of Monster Hunters | Includes bibliographical references and index. | Audience: Ages 10-13. | Audience: Grades 4-6. | Summary: Amy, Elena, and Jorge travel to Harlem in 1928 to rescue a fairy trapped in a jazz club.
Identifiers: LCCN 2020016498 (print) | LCCN 2020016499 (ebook) | ISBN 9781534169388 (hardcover) | ISBN 9781534171060 (paperback) | ISBN 9781534172906 (pdf) | ISBN 9781534174740 (ebook)
Subjects: LCSH: Graphic novels. | CYAC: Graphic novels. | Fairies—Fiction. | Time travel—Fiction. | Secret societies—Fiction. | Harlem (New York, N.Y.)—History—20th century—Fiction. | New York (State)—History—20th century—Fiction.
Classification: LCC PZ7.7.K355 Fai 2020 (print) | LCC PZ7.7.K355 (ebook) | DDC 741.5/973—dc23
LC record available at https://lccn.loc.gov/2020016498
LC ebook record available at https://lccn.loc.gov/2020016499

Cherry Lake Publishing Group would like to acknowledge the work of the Partnership for 21st Century Learning, a Network of Battelle for Kids. Please visit http://www.battelleforkids.org/networks/p21 for more information.

Printed in the United States of America
Corporate Graphics

TABLE OF CONTENTS

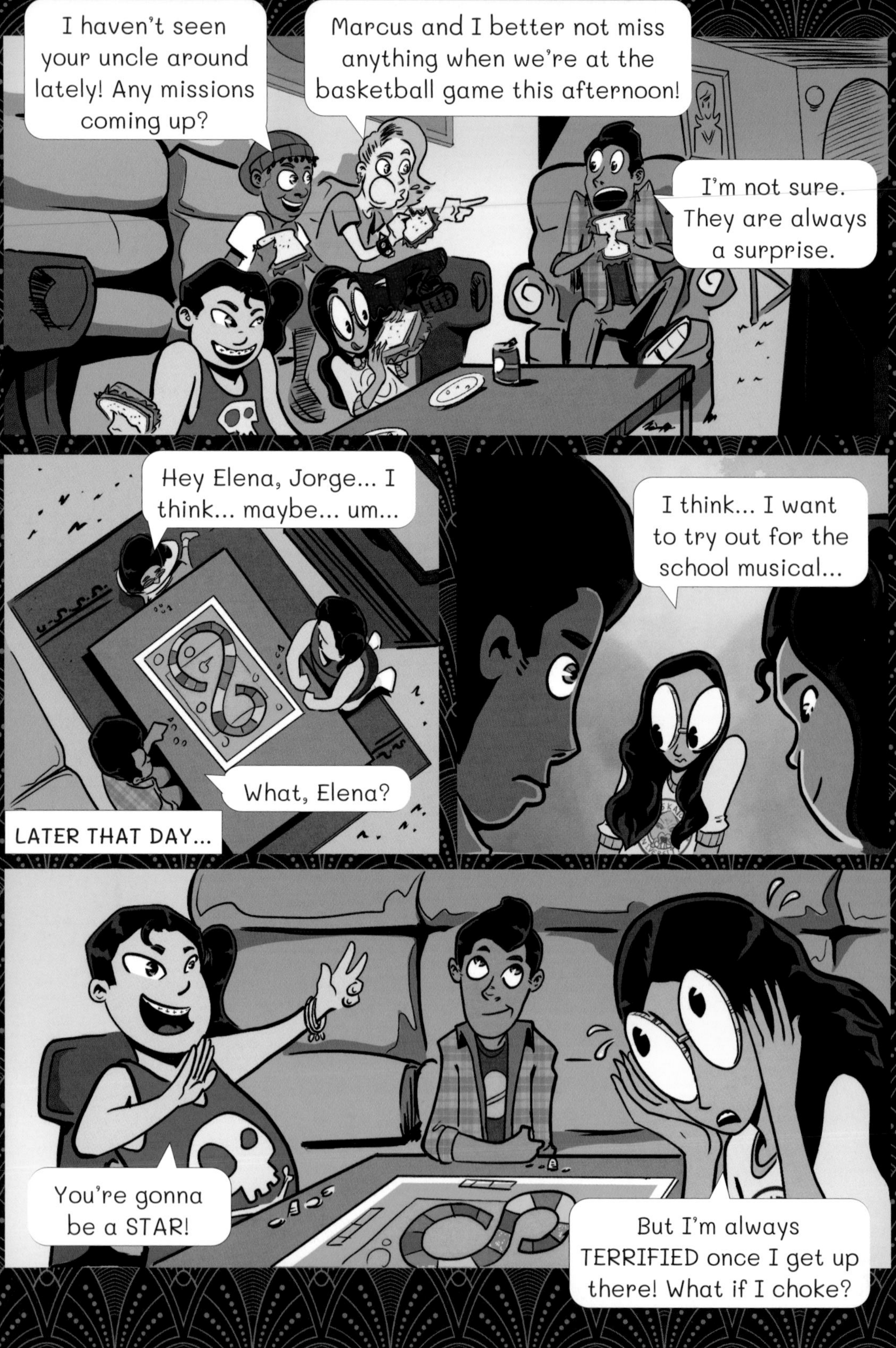
I haven't seen your uncle around lately! Any missions coming up?
Marcus and I better not miss anything when we're at the basketball game this afternoon!
I'm not sure. They are always a surprise.
LATER THAT DAY...
Hey Elena, Jorge... I think... maybe... um...
What, Elena?
I think... I want to try out for the school musical...
You're gonna be a STAR!
But I'm always TERRIFIED once I get up there! What if I choke?

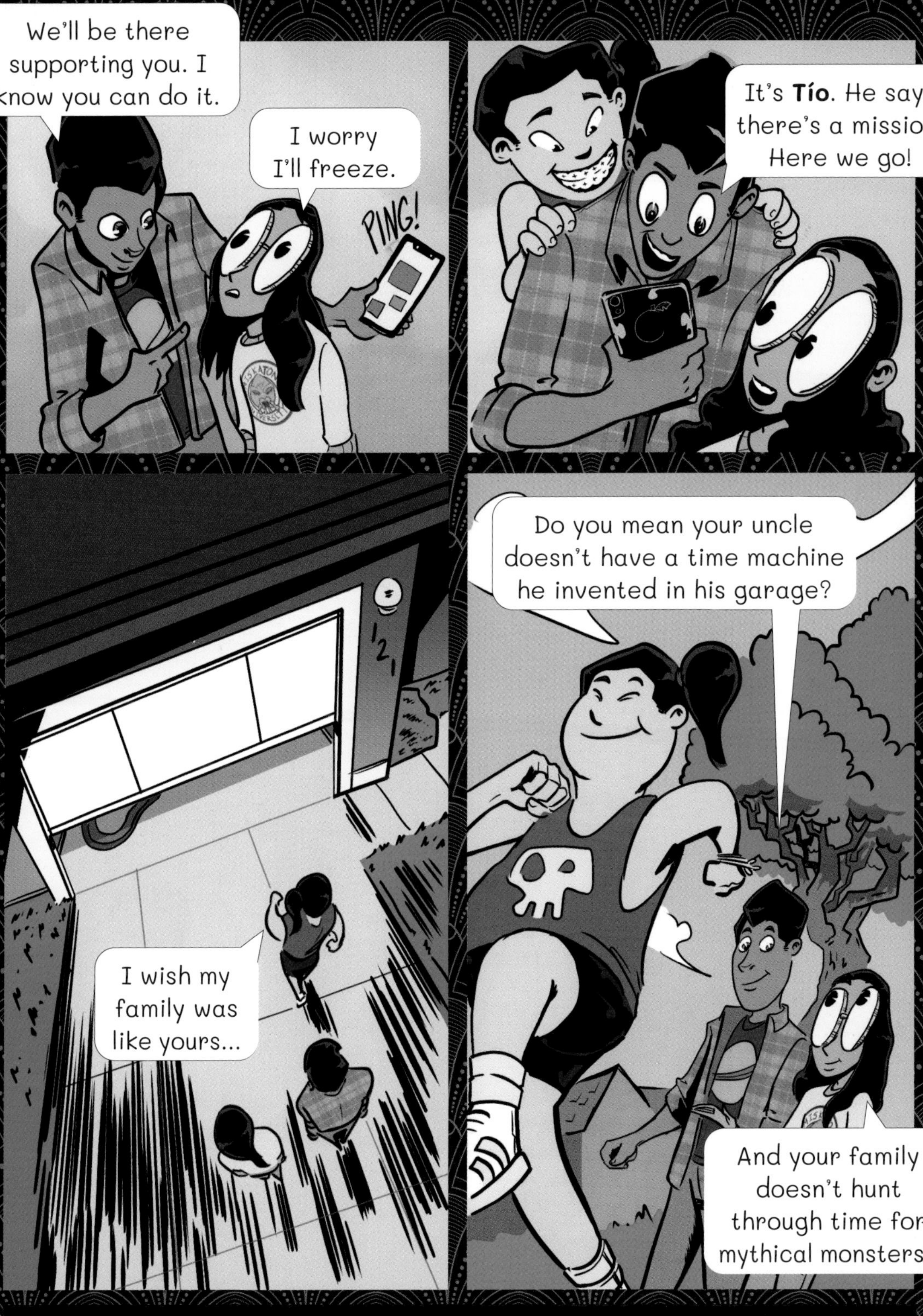
We'll be there supporting you. I know you can do it.
I worry I'll freeze.
PING!
It's **Tío**. He says there's a mission. Here we go!
I wish my family was like yours...
Do you mean your uncle doesn't have a time machine he invented in his garage?
And your family doesn't hunt through time for mythical monsters?

tío: "uncle" in Spanish

Okay, kiddos. Here's the deal. A powerful fairy was sighted in New York.

Wait, what?! Let me check online!

No, no, no. This was in the 1920s. All I know is, she was captured and held captive in Harlem. Then, she disappeared entirely during the **Great Depression**.

You will need to travel to 1928 and find her. We can't let her be found out. Fairy magic can be dangerous in the wrong hands.

Sure, Tío!

Okay, but first, there's a lot more to know about fairies than you might think...

Great Depression: a financial slump in the United States that started in 1929

TIPS FOR THE DECADE

During the Roaring Twenties, also called the Jazz Age, the United States was a new and proud world power after winning World War I.

* Women gained the right to vote in 1920.

* The **economy** was growing! People could suddenly afford luxury items, like cars and radios. People loved to go out to eat, drink, and dance.

* Harlem was the center of New York jazz. African American musicians thrived during this time.

* Jazz was one part of a great art movement called the Harlem **Renaissance**. Giants of writing, music, and theater were all working in Harlem at the same time.

By the end of the 1920s, the Great Depression gripped America, dampening the "roar" of the 20s.

economy: The system of making and using money in a particular location

renaissance: a rebirth of art and culture

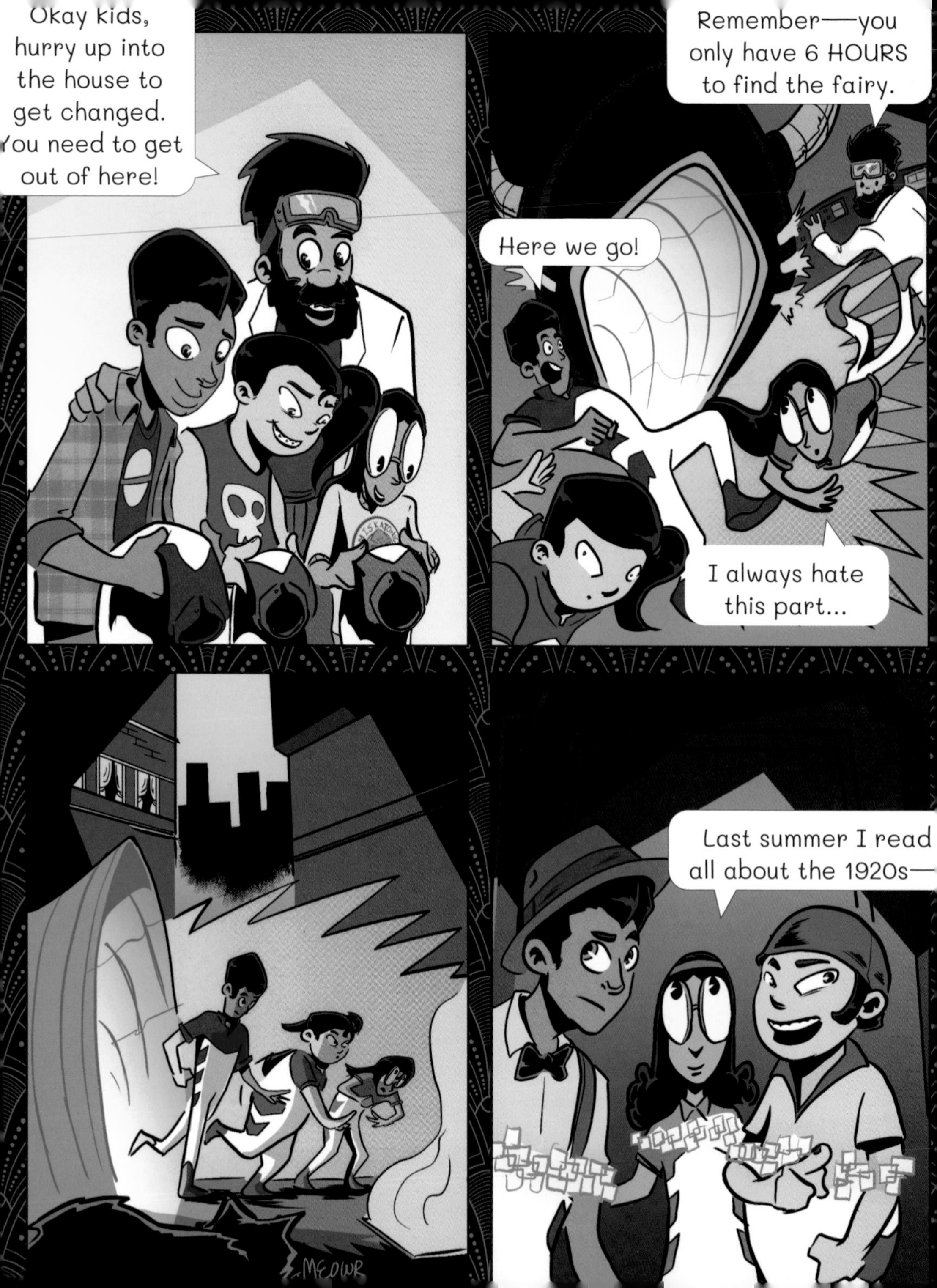
Okay kids, hurry up into the house to get changed. You need to get out of here!
Remember—you only have 6 HOURS to find the fairy.
Here we go!
I always hate this part...
MEOWR
Last summer I read all about the 1920s—

PACKING LIST

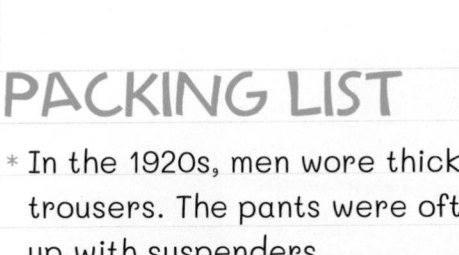

* In the 1920s, men wore thick, baggy trousers. The pants were often held up with suspenders.

* Men also wore button-up shirts, vests, and ties.

* Women often wore dresses. They were low waisted and loose fitting.

* Flappers wore beaded dresses and headbands. These were sometimes decorated with feathers.

* Hats were necessary for everyone when they were outside. Women wore close-fitting cloche hats. Men wore dashing fedora hats.

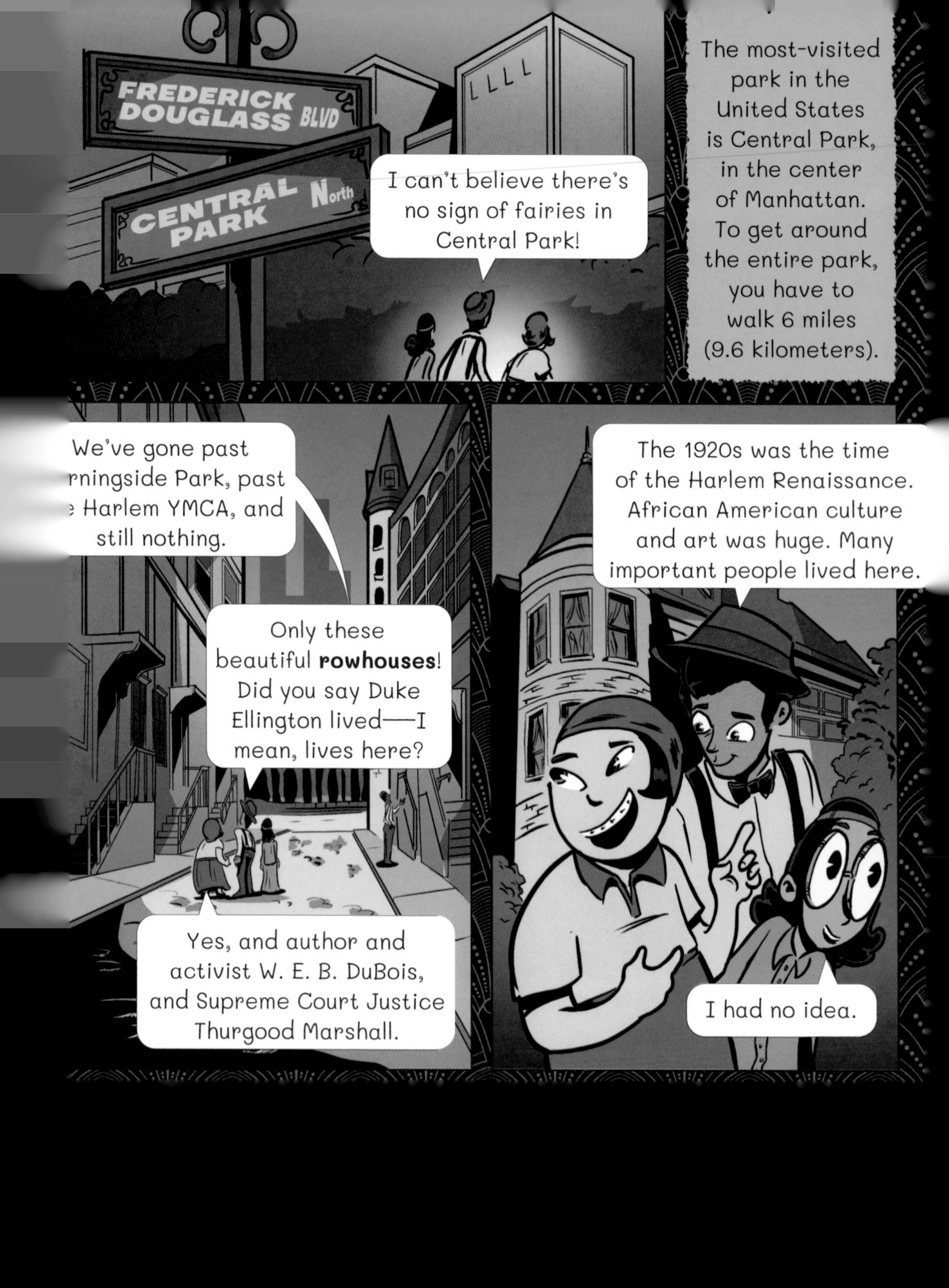
FREDERICK DOUGLASS BLVD
CENTRAL PARK North
I can't believe there's no sign of fairies in Central Park!
The most-visited park in the United States is Central Park, in the center of Manhattan. To get around the entire park, you have to walk 6 miles (9.6 kilometers).
We've gone past rningside Park, past e Harlem YMCA, and still nothing.
Only these beautiful **rowhouses**! Did you say Duke Ellington lived—I mean, lives here?
Yes, and author and activist W. E. B. DuBois, and Supreme Court Justice Thurgood Marshall.
The 1920s was the time of the Harlem Renaissance. African American culture and art was huge. Many important people lived here.
I had no idea.

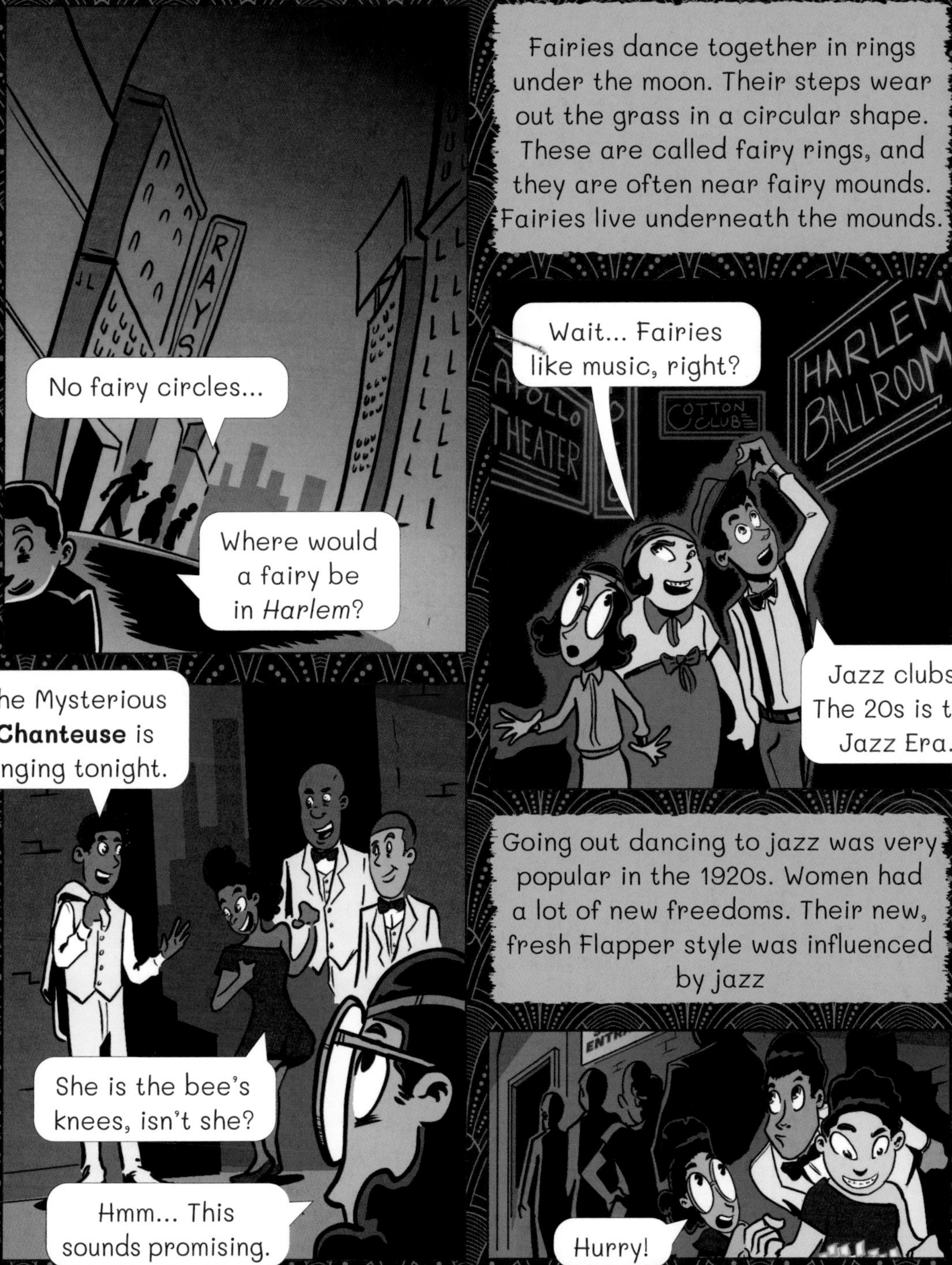
No fairy circles...
Where would a fairy be in *Harlem*?
Fairies dance together in rings under the moon. Their steps wear out the grass in a circular shape. These are called fairy rings, and they are often near fairy mounds. Fairies live underneath the mounds.
Wait... Fairies like music, right?
HARLEM BALLROOM
APOLLO THEATER
COTTON CLUB
Jazz clubs. The 20s is the Jazz Era.
The Mysterious **Chanteuse** is singing tonight.
She is the bee's knees, isn't she?
Hmm... This sounds promising.
Going out dancing to jazz was very popular in the 1920s. Women had a lot of new freedoms. Their new, fresh Flapper style was influenced by jazz
Hurry!

chanteuse: a female singer, espeically one who sings in nightclubs

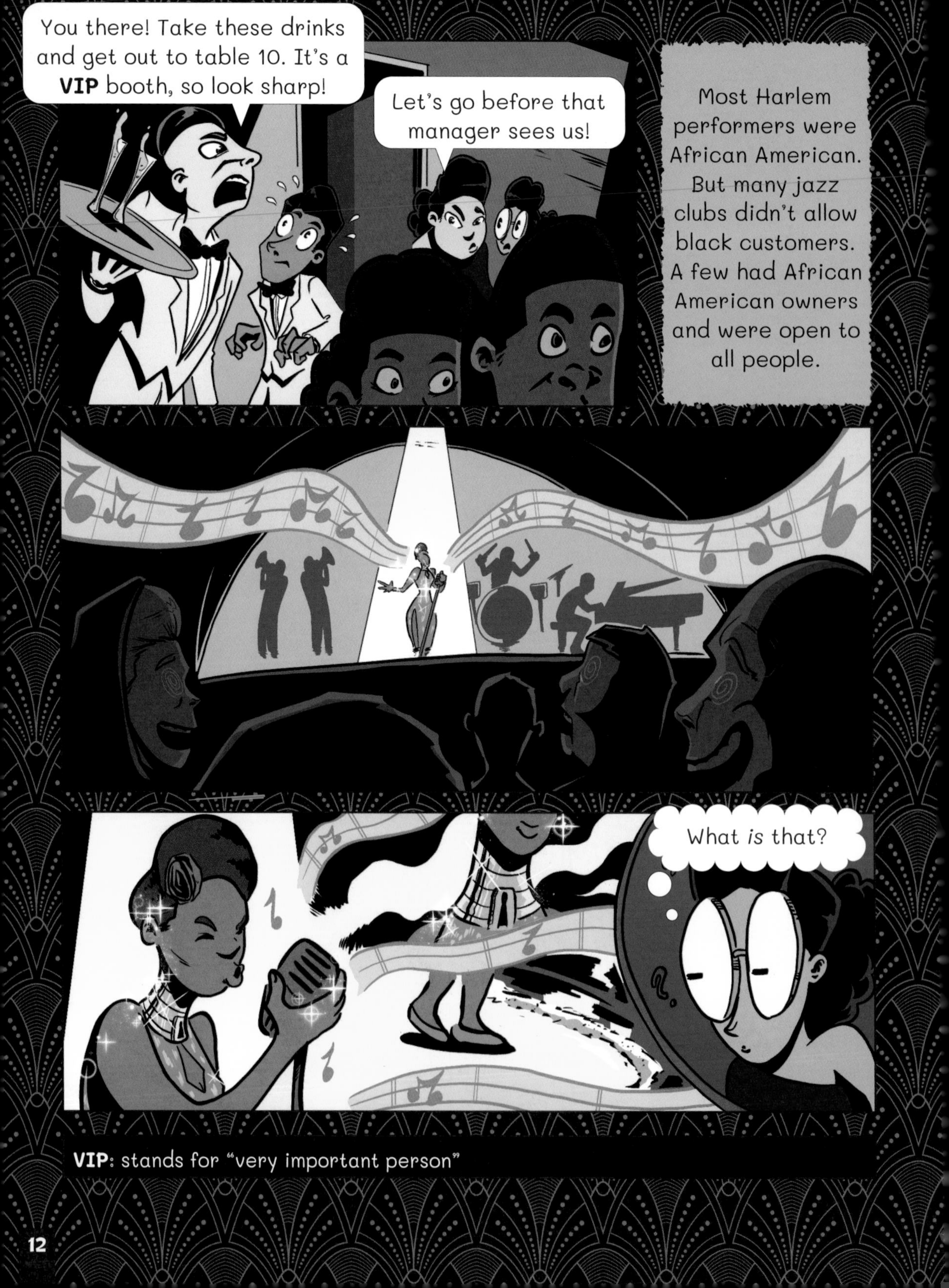
You there! Take these drinks and get out to table 10. It's a **VIP** booth, so look sharp!
Let's go before that manager sees us!
Most Harlem performers were African American. But many jazz clubs didn't allow black customers. A few had African American owners and were open to all people.
What *is* that?

VIP: stands for "very important person"

WHAT ARE FAIRIES?

No one knows where fairies came from. They could be **ancient** humans. They could be fallen angels. This is a list of what is known.

* They live for a very long time.

* It's important to be careful around them. Fairies can be tricky.

* They have their own **realm**, but they can live among humans.

* They can change how they look. You can't always tell if someone is a fairy.

* Fairies love children. They also love nature, music, and dancing.

* Their music is enchanting to humans.

* Fairies value kindness and good manners. They hate lying.

* They love bright, sparkling objects like crystal jewelry.

* A fairy's favorite colors are green and red.

* A fairy's weakness is iron. Iron stops their magic.

* Fairies can be trapped inside a circle of salt. Some say this is because fairies must stop and count every grain of salt. Some say it is because salt is **sacred**.

ancient: very, very old
realm: a kingdom or land
sacred: respected by a particular group or individual

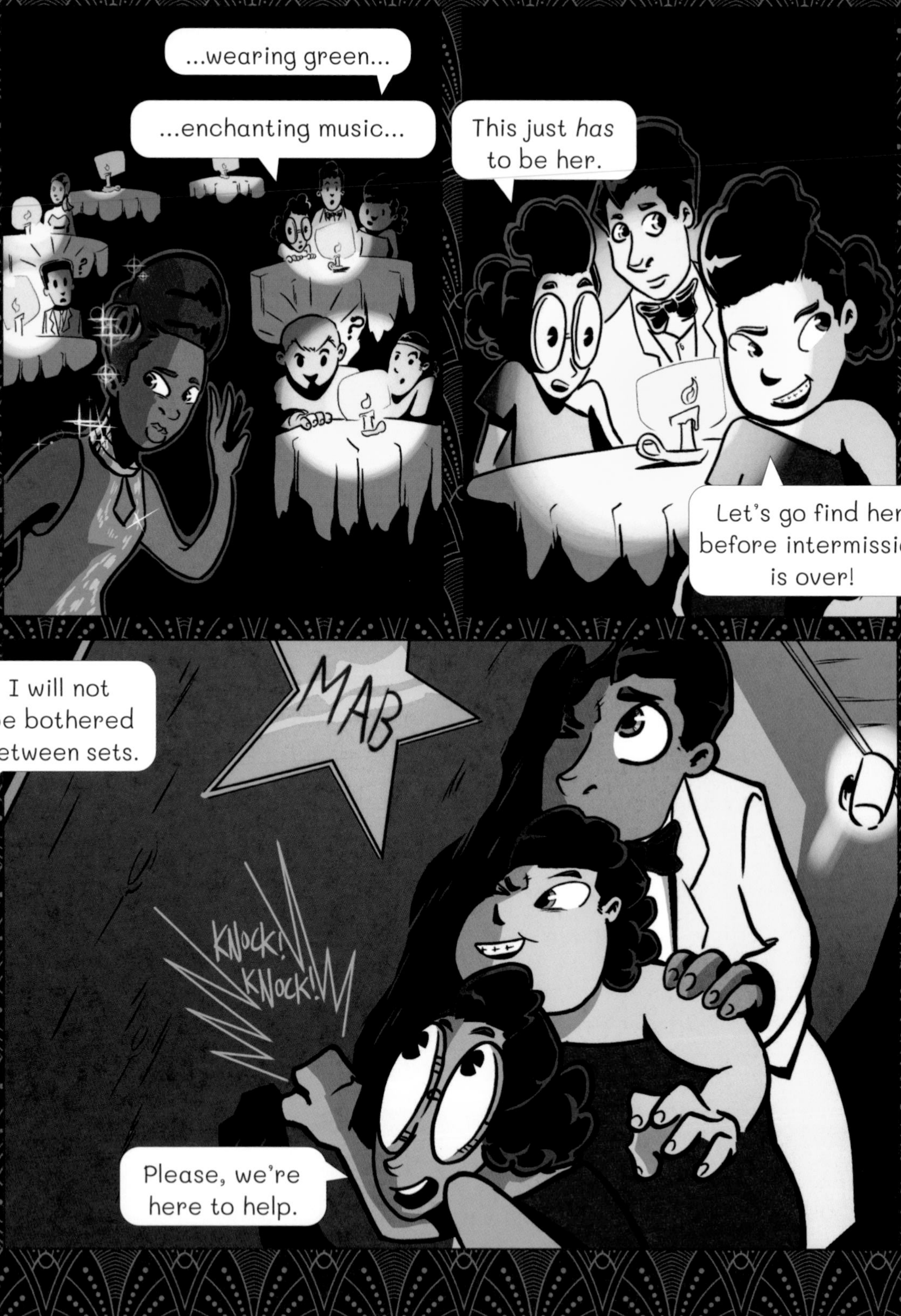
...wearing green...
...enchanting music...
This just *has* to be her.
Let's go find her before intermission is over!
I will not be bothered between sets.
MAB
KNOCK! KNOCK!
Please, we're here to help.

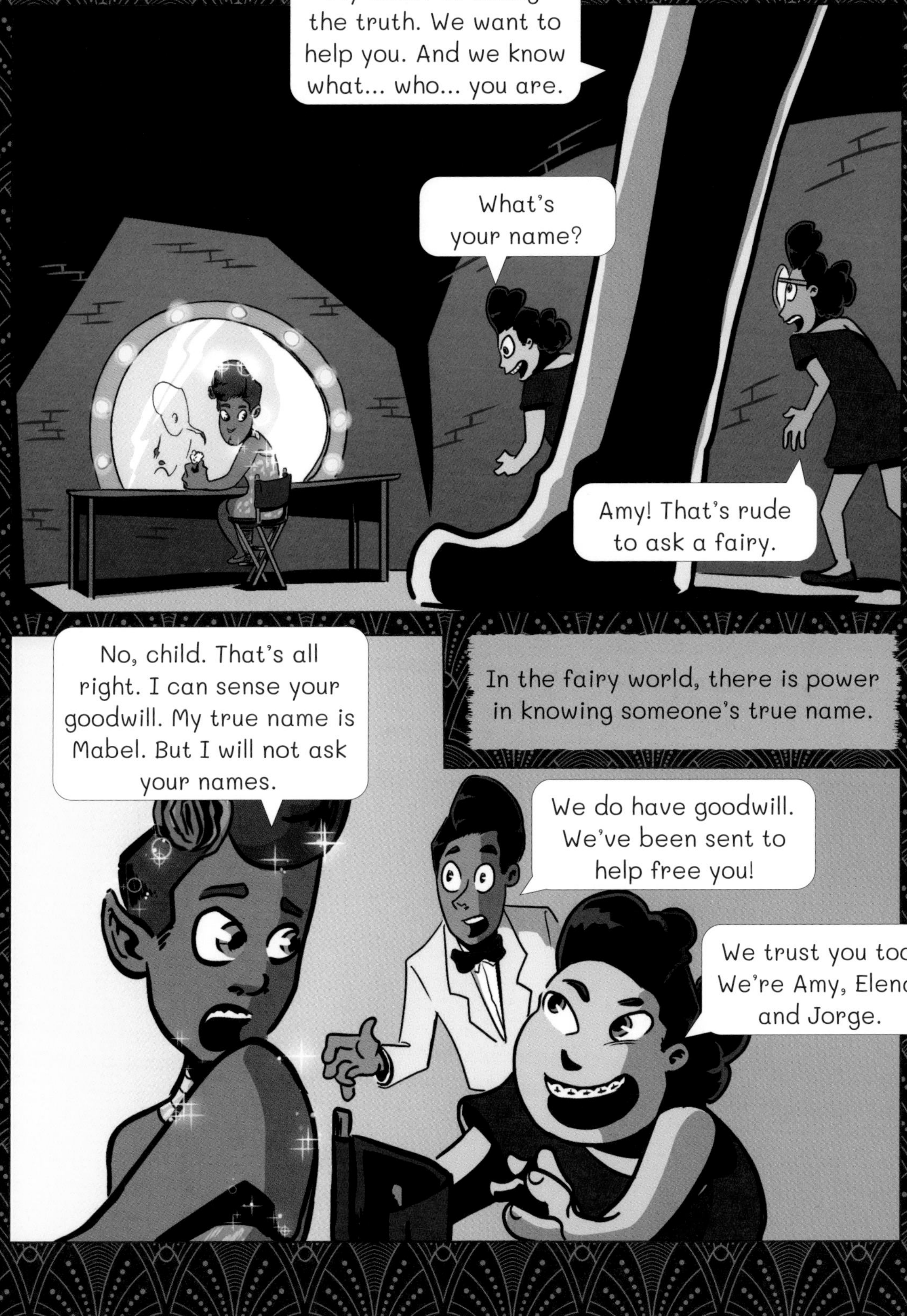
My sister is telling the truth. We want to help you. And we know what... who... you are.
What's your name?
Amy! That's rude to ask a fairy.
No, child. That's all right. I can sense your goodwill. My true name is Mabel. But I will not ask your names.
In the fairy world, there is power in knowing someone's true name.
We do have goodwill. We've been sent to help free you!
We trust you too! We're Amy, Elena, and Jorge.

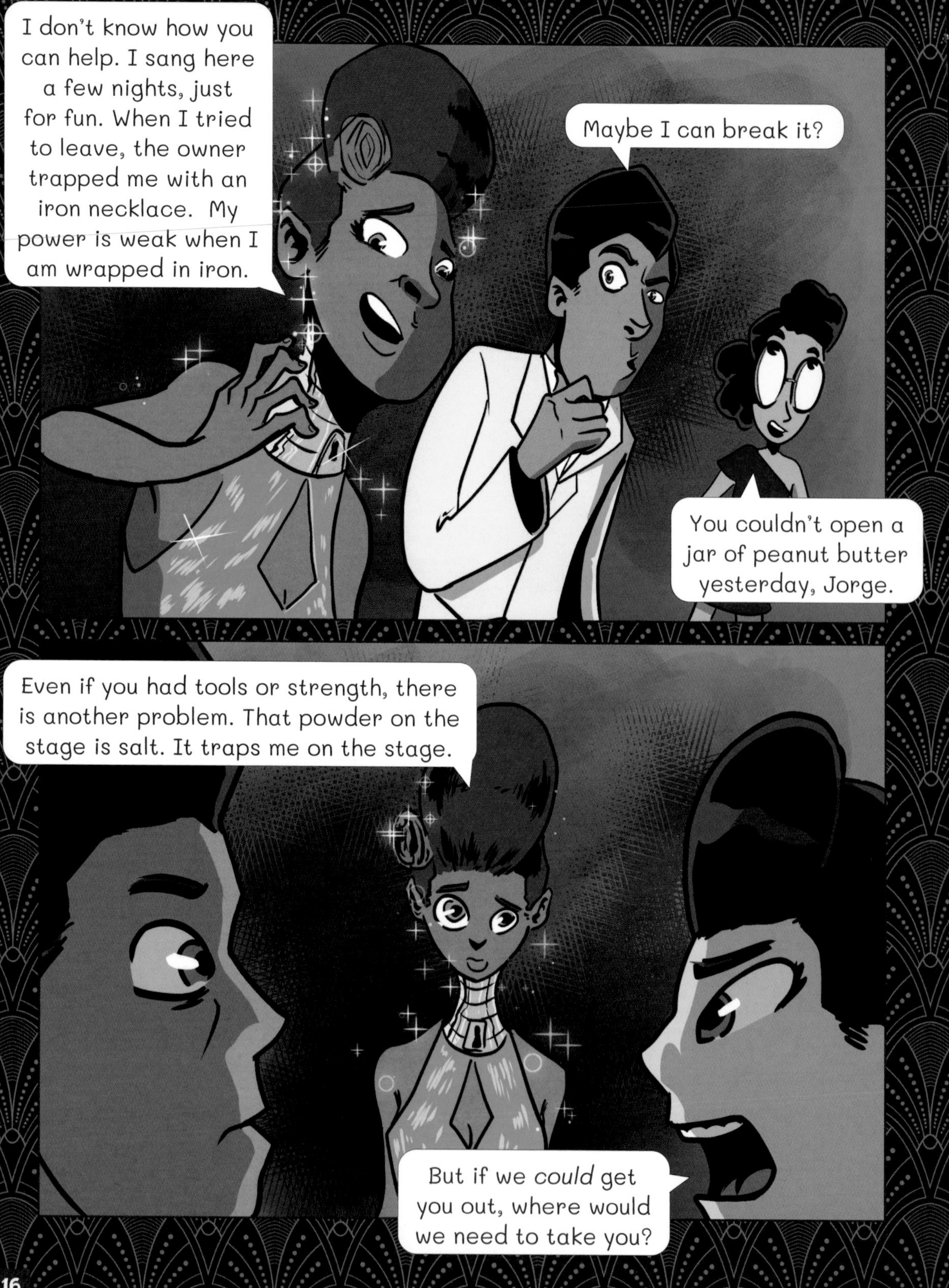
I don't know how you can help. I sang here a few nights, just for fun. When I tried to leave, the owner trapped me with an iron necklace. My power is weak when I am wrapped in iron.
Maybe I can break it?
You couldn't open a jar of peanut butter yesterday, Jorge.
Even if you had tools or strength, there is another problem. That powder on the stage is salt. It traps me on the stage.
But if we *could* get you out, where would we need to take you?

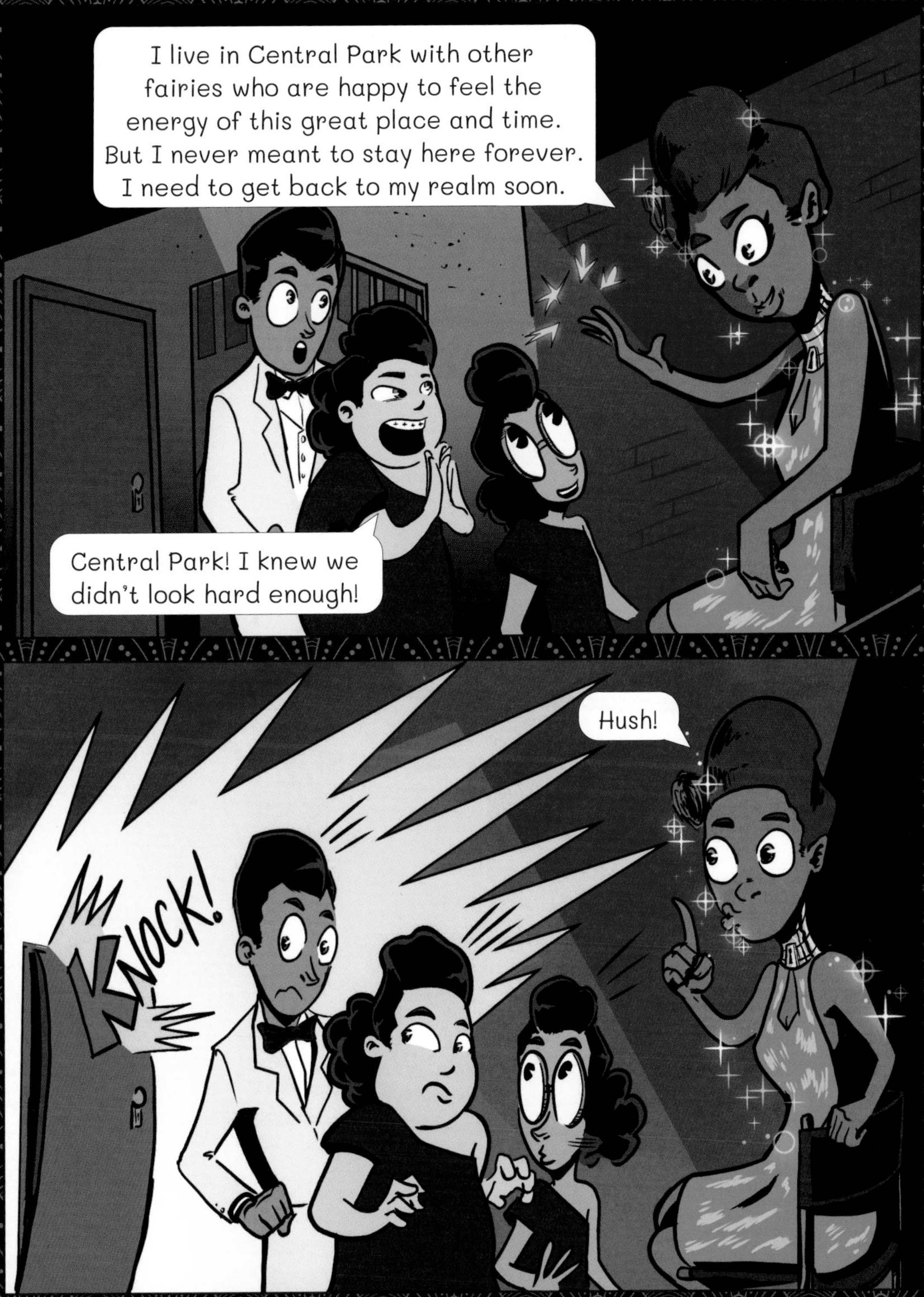
I live in Central Park with other fairies who are happy to feel the energy of this great place and time. But I never meant to stay here forever. I need to get back to my realm soon.
Central Park! I knew we didn't look hard enough!
KNOCK!
Hush!

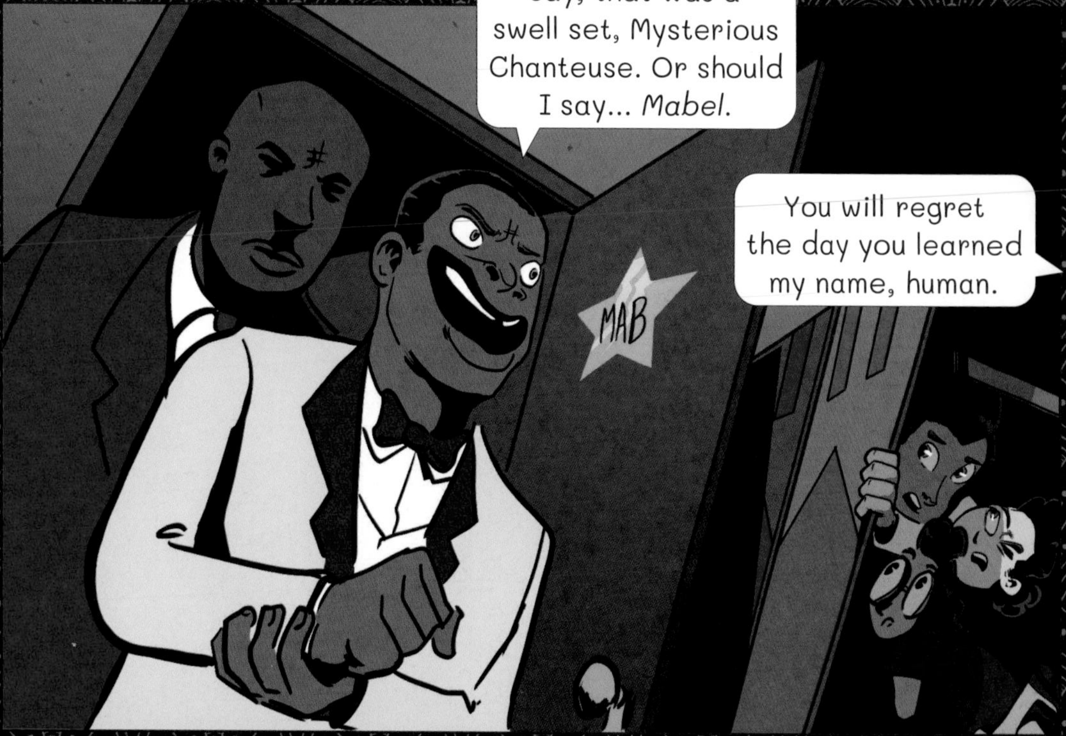
Say, that was a swell set, Mysterious Chanteuse. Or should I say... *Mabel*.
MAB
You will regret the day you learned my name, human.

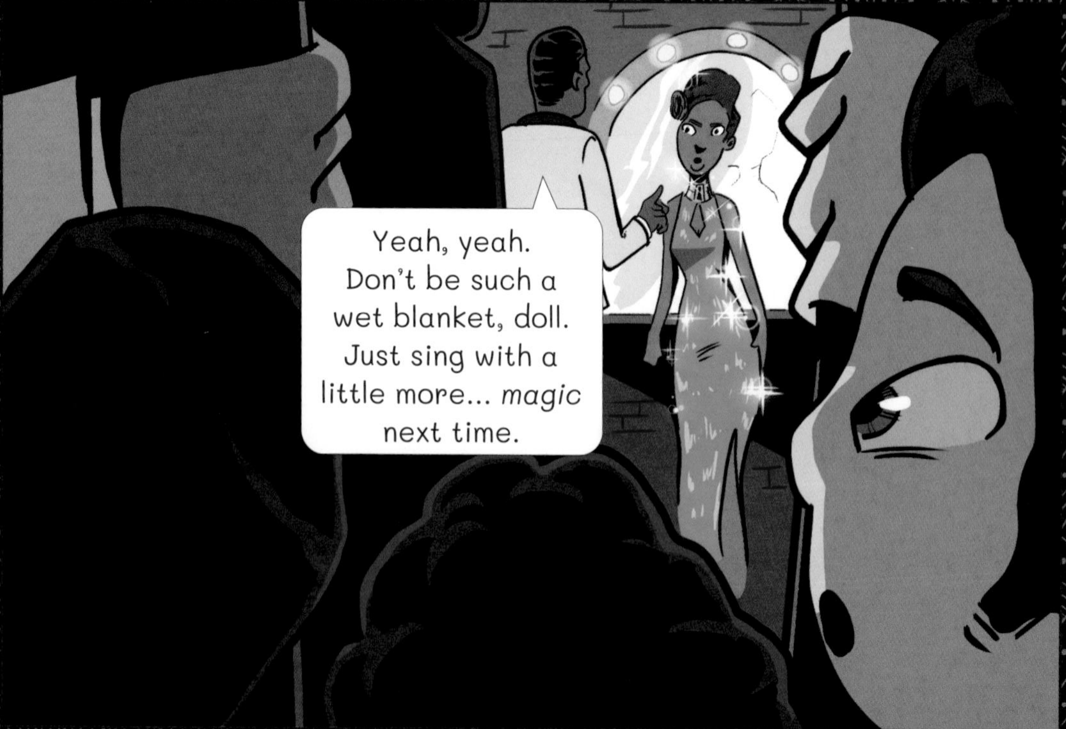
Yeah, yeah. Don't be such a wet blanket, doll. Just sing with a little more... *magic* next time.

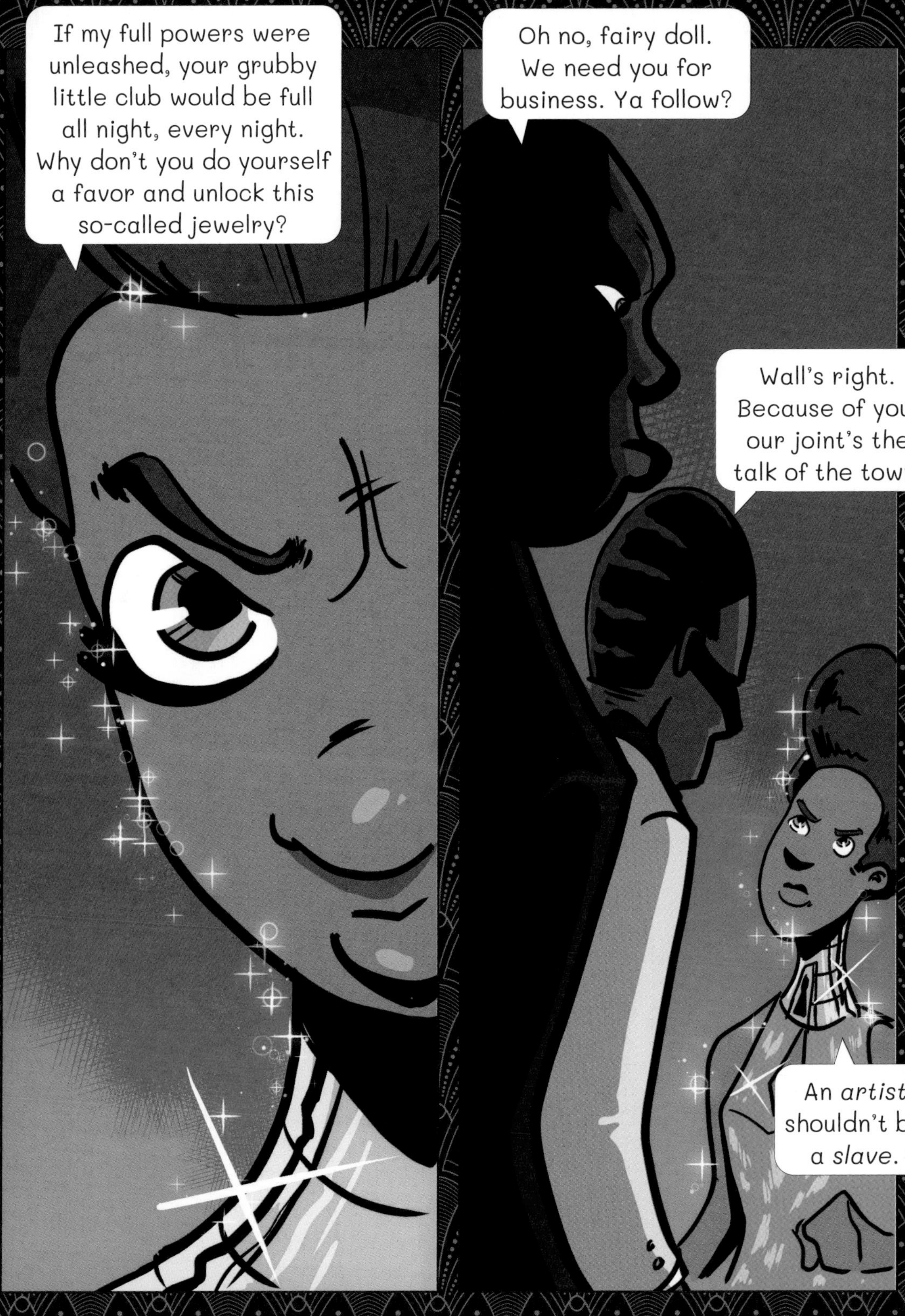
If my full powers were unleashed, your grubby little club would be full all night, every night. Why don't you do yourself a favor and unlock this so-called jewelry?
Oh no, fairy doll. We need you for business. Ya follow?
Wall's right. Because of you, our joint's the talk of the town!
An *artist* shouldn't be a *slave*.

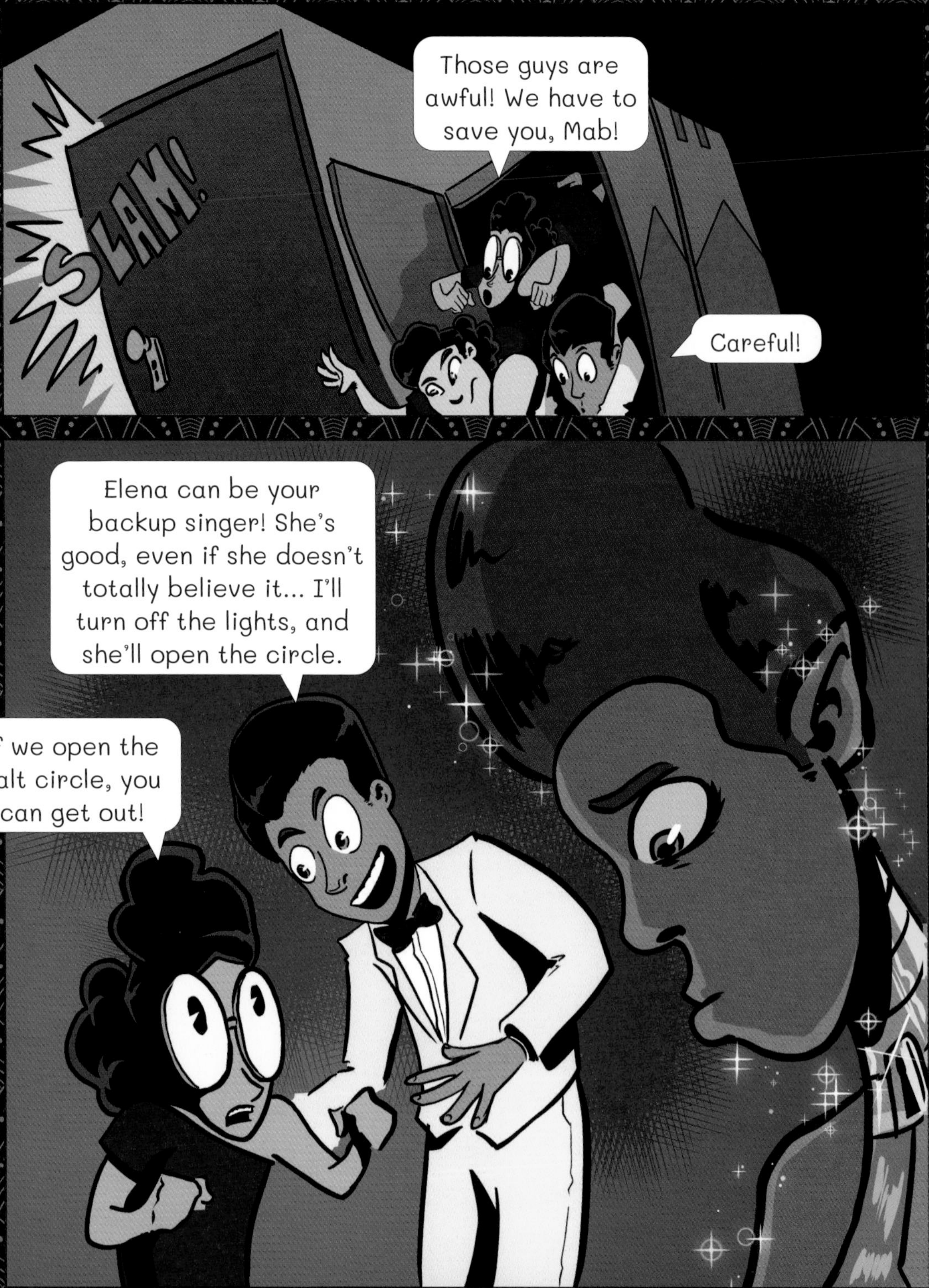
SLAM!
Those guys are awful! We have to save you, Mab!
Careful!
Elena can be your backup singer! She's good, even if she doesn't totally believe it... I'll turn off the lights, and she'll open the circle.
If we open the salt circle, you can get out!

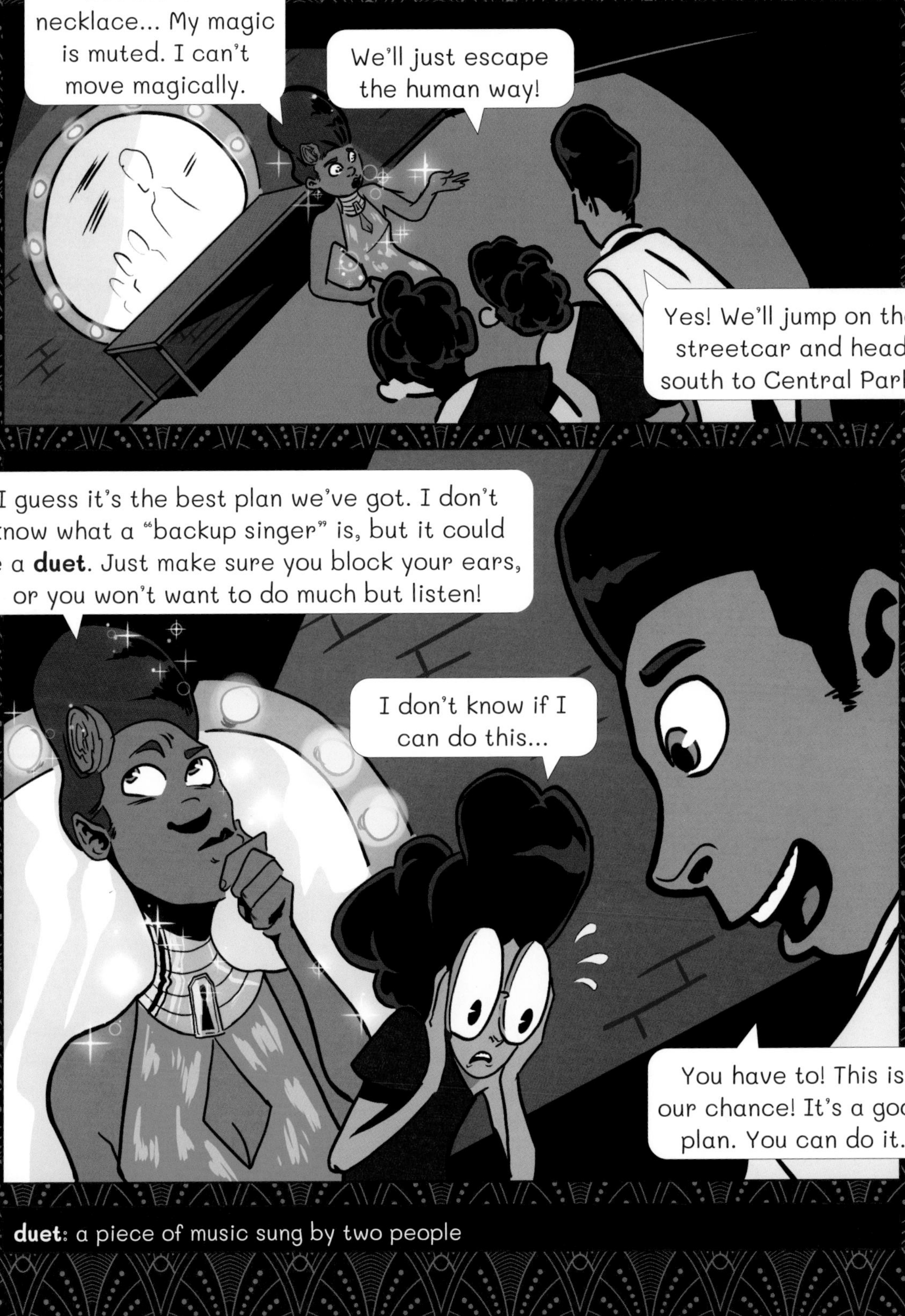
But the iron necklace... My magic is muted. I can't move magically.
We'll just escape the human way!
Yes! We'll jump on the streetcar and head south to Central Park.
I guess it's the best plan we've got. I don't know what a "backup singer" is, but it could be a **duet**. Just make sure you block your ears, or you won't want to do much but listen!
I don't know if I can do this...
You have to! This is our chance! It's a good plan. You can do it.

duet: a piece of music sung by two people

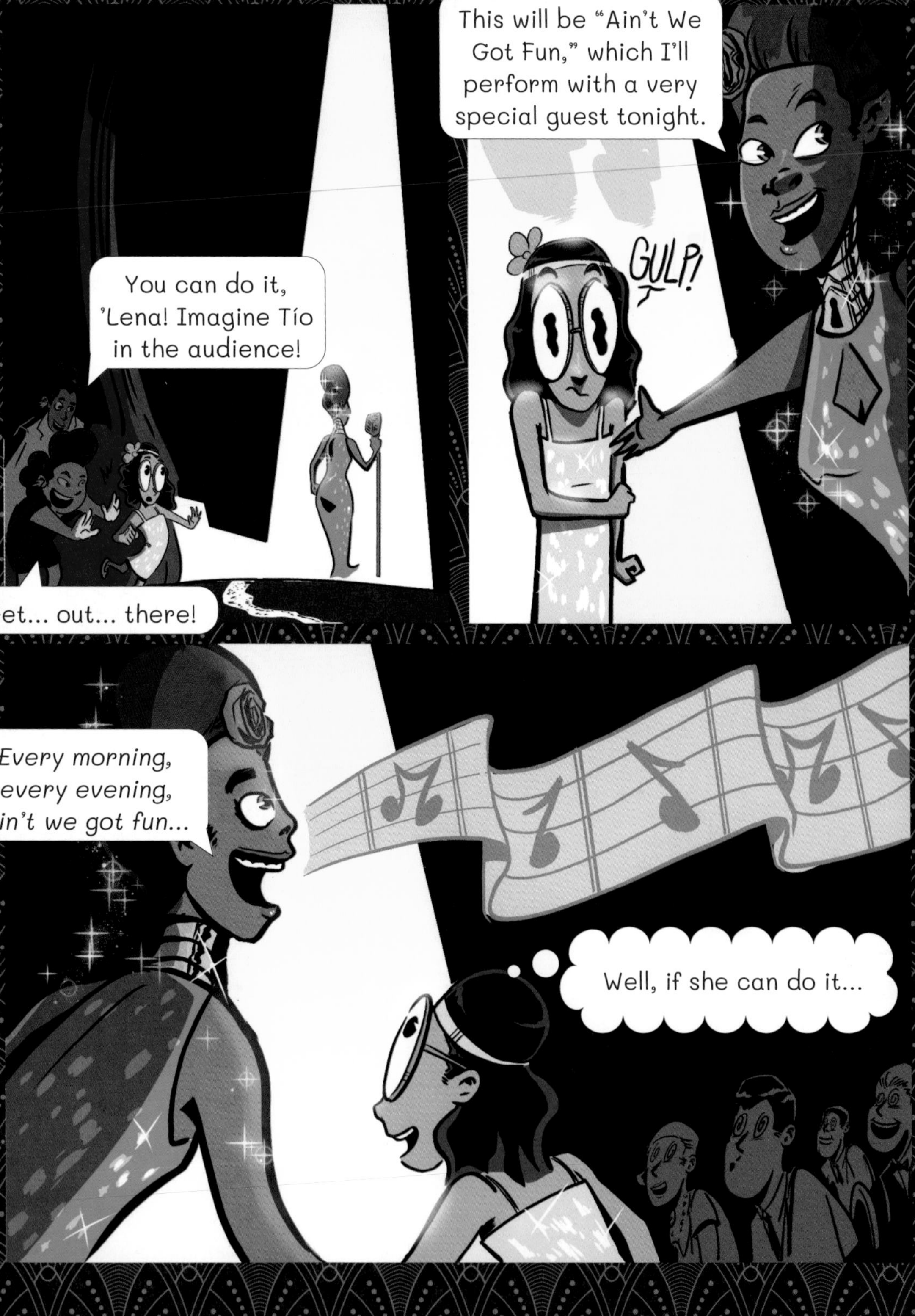
You can do it, 'Lena! Imagine Tío in the audience!
Get... out... there!
This will be "Ain't We Got Fun," which I'll perform with a very special guest tonight.
GULP!
Every morning, every evening, ain't we got fun...
Well, if she can do it...

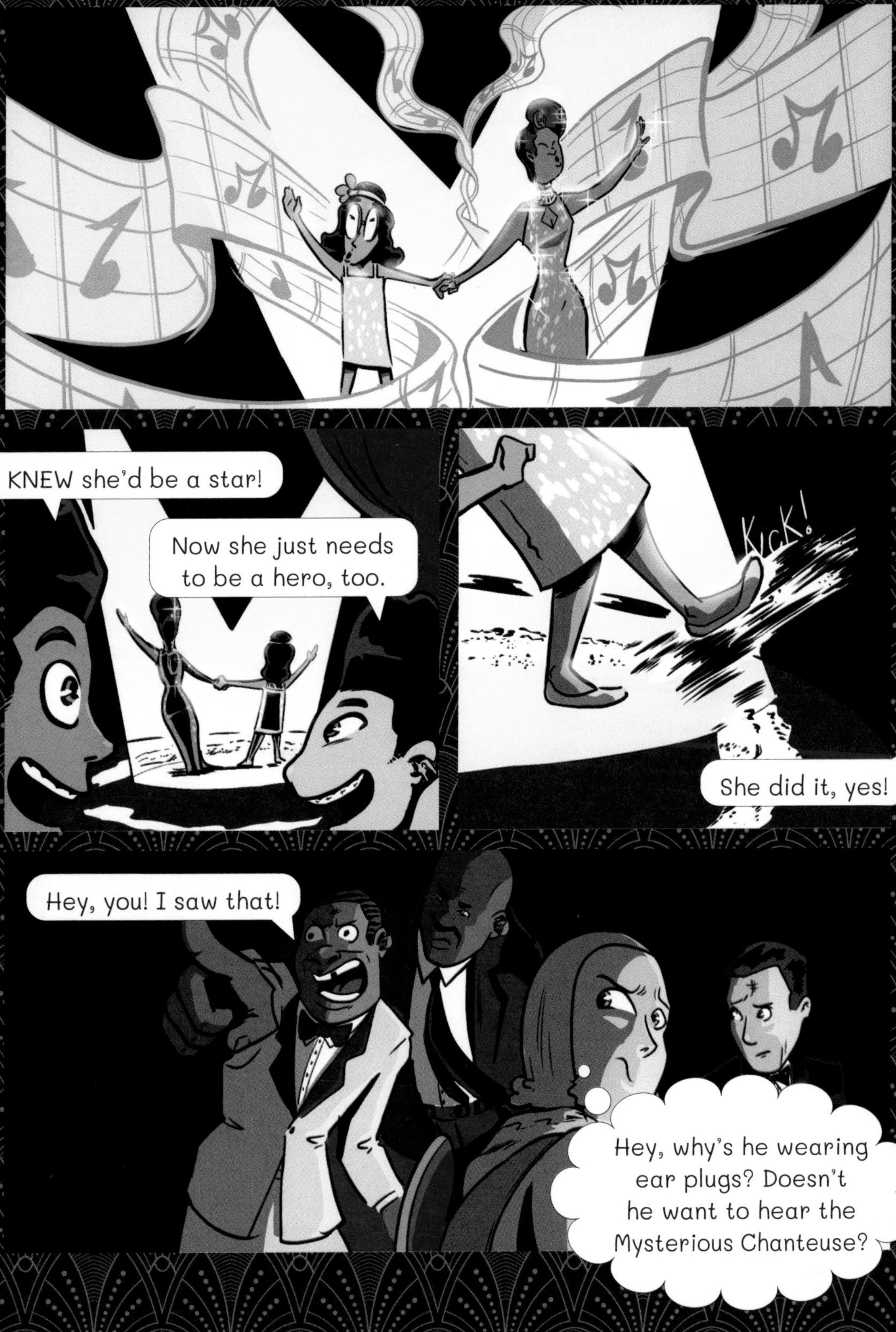
I KNEW she'd be a star!
Now she just needs to be a hero, too.
KICK!
She did it, yes!
Hey, you! I saw that!
Hey, why's he wearing ear plugs? Doesn't he want to hear the Mysterious Chanteuse?

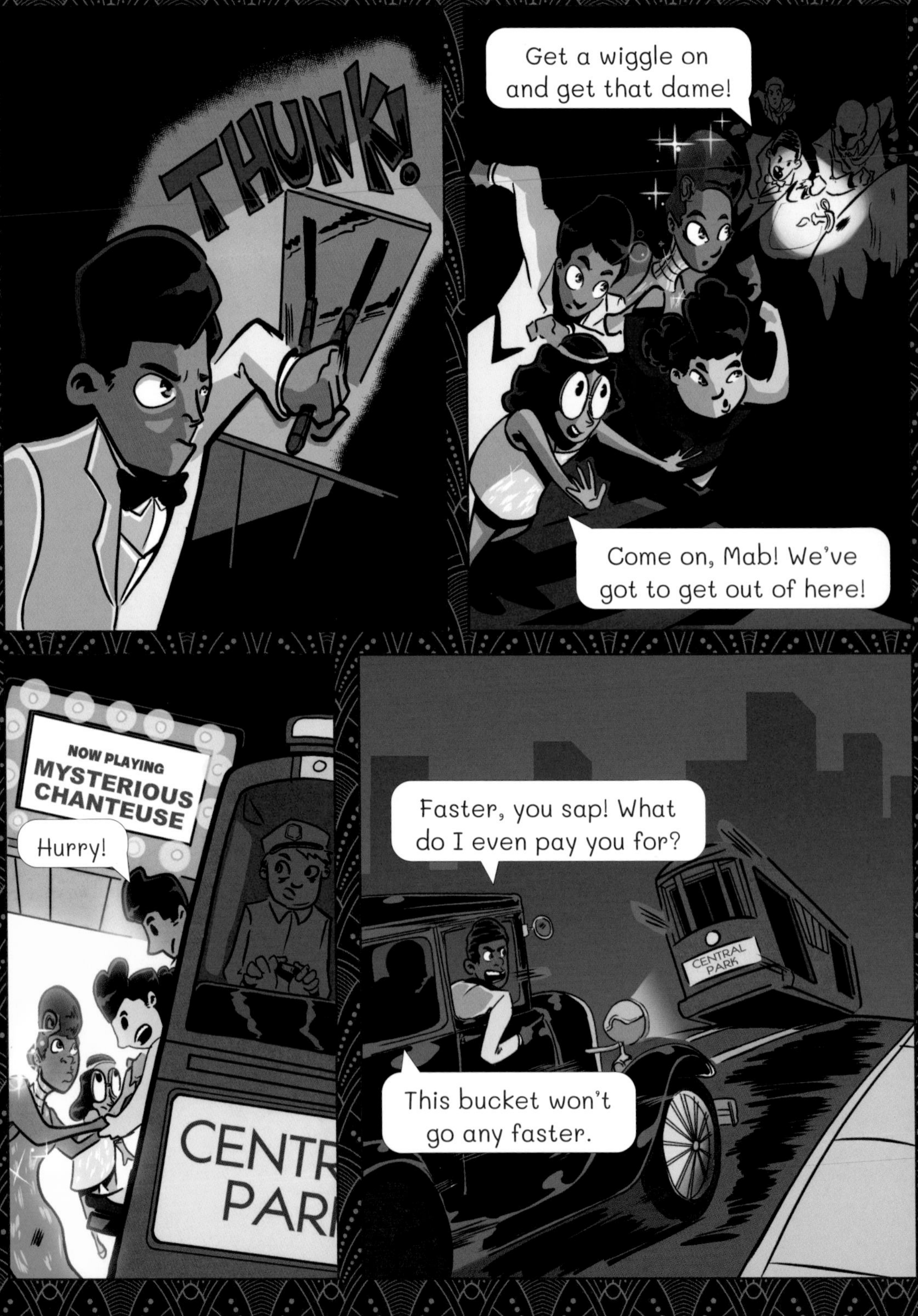
THUNK!
Get a wiggle on and get that dame!
Come on, Mab! We've got to get out of here!
NOW PLAYING MYSTERIOUS CHANTEUSE
Hurry!
CENTR PARI
Faster, you sap! What do I even pay you for?
CENTRAL PARK
This bucket won't go any faster.

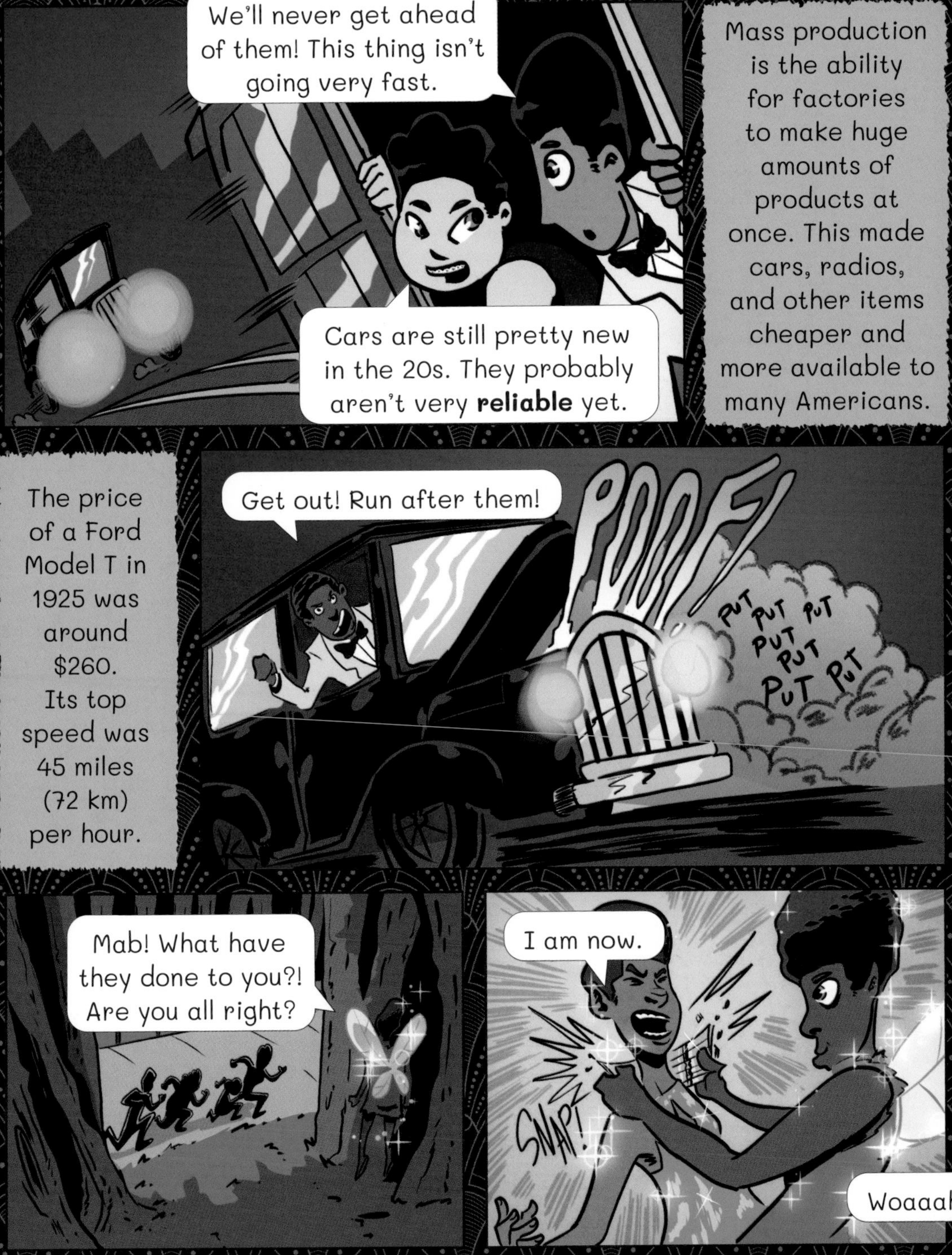
We'll never get ahead of them! This thing isn't going very fast.
Cars are still pretty new in the 20s. They probably aren't very **reliable** yet.
Mass production is the ability for factories to make huge amounts of products at once. This made cars, radios, and other items cheaper and more available to many Americans.
The price of a Ford Model T in 1925 was around $260. Its top speed was 45 miles (72 km) per hour.
Get out! Run after them!
POOF!
PUT PUT PUT PUT PUT PUT PUT
Mab! What have they done to you?! Are you all right?
I am now.
SNAP!
Woaaah!

reliable: able to be trusted

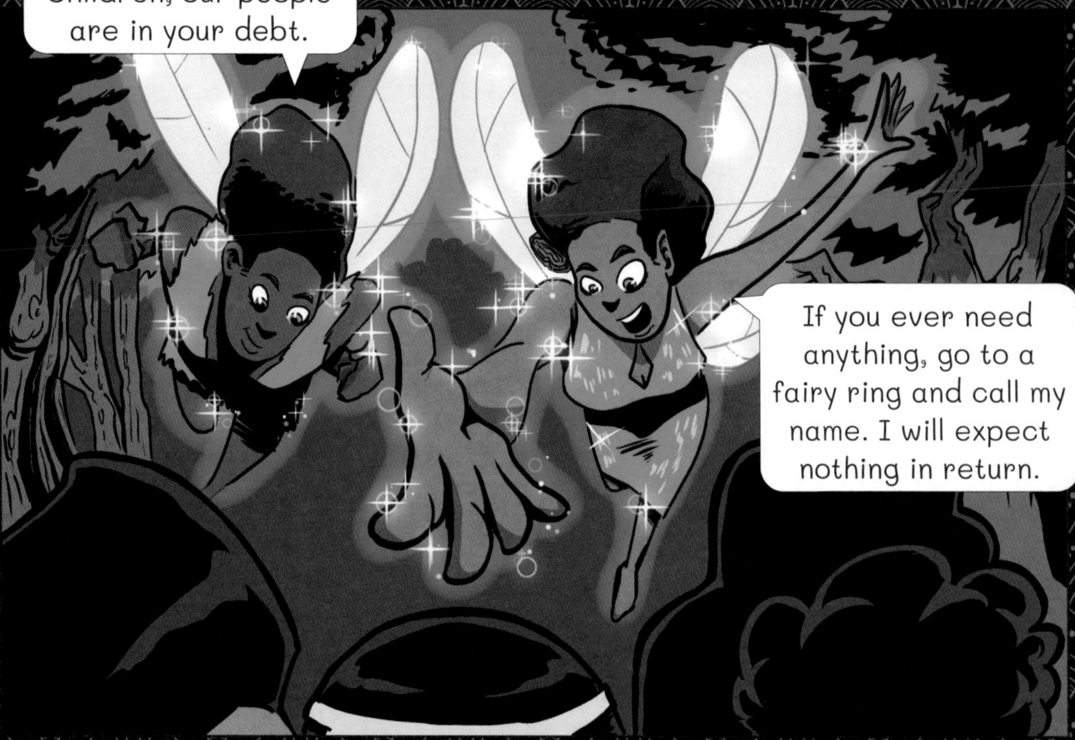
Children, our people are in your debt.
If you ever need anything, go to a fairy ring and call my name. I will expect nothing in return.

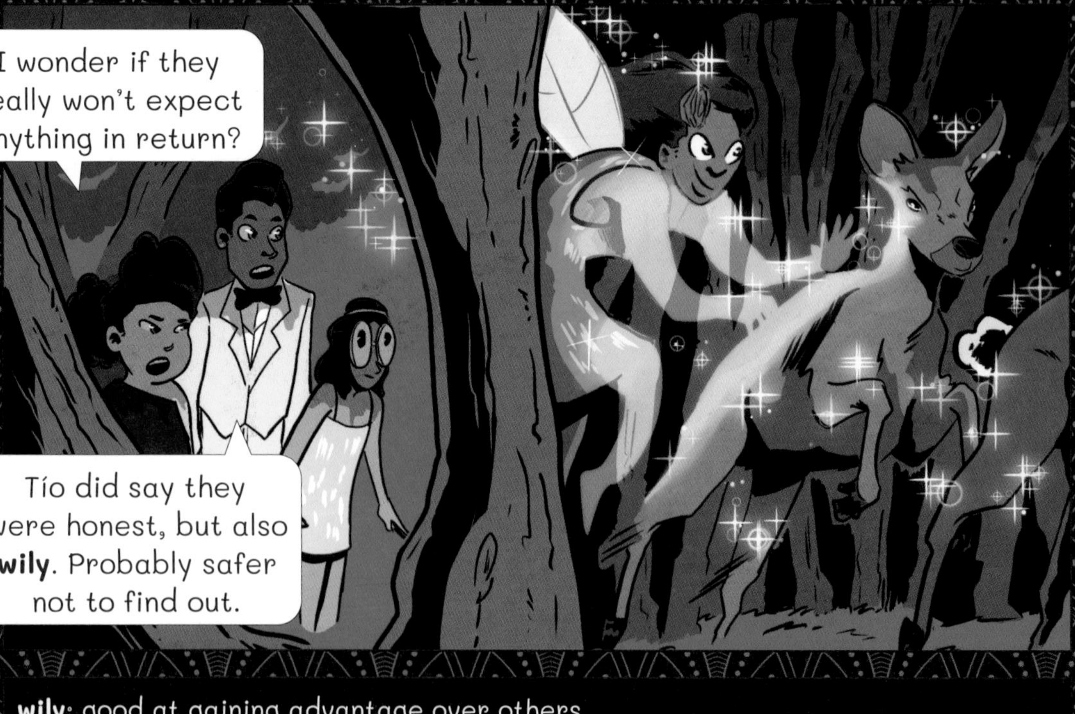
I wonder if they really won't expect anything in return?
Tío did say they were honest, but also **wily**. Probably safer not to find out.

wily: good at gaining advantage over others

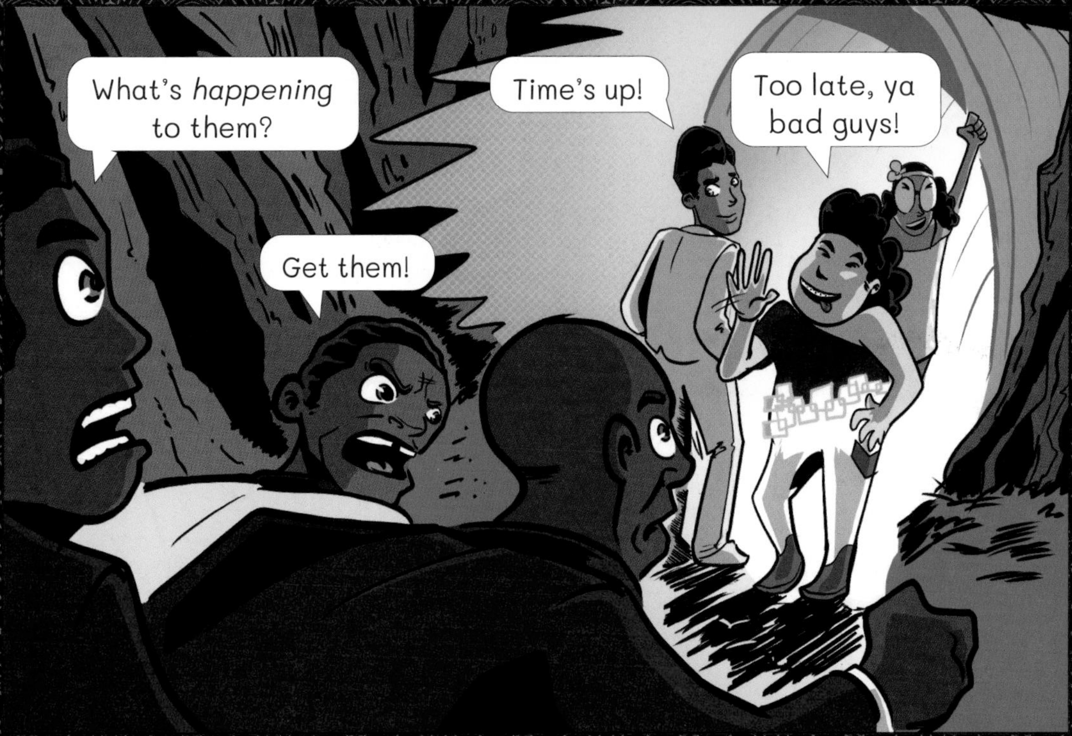
What's *happening* to them?
Time's up!
Too late, ya bad guys!
Get them!

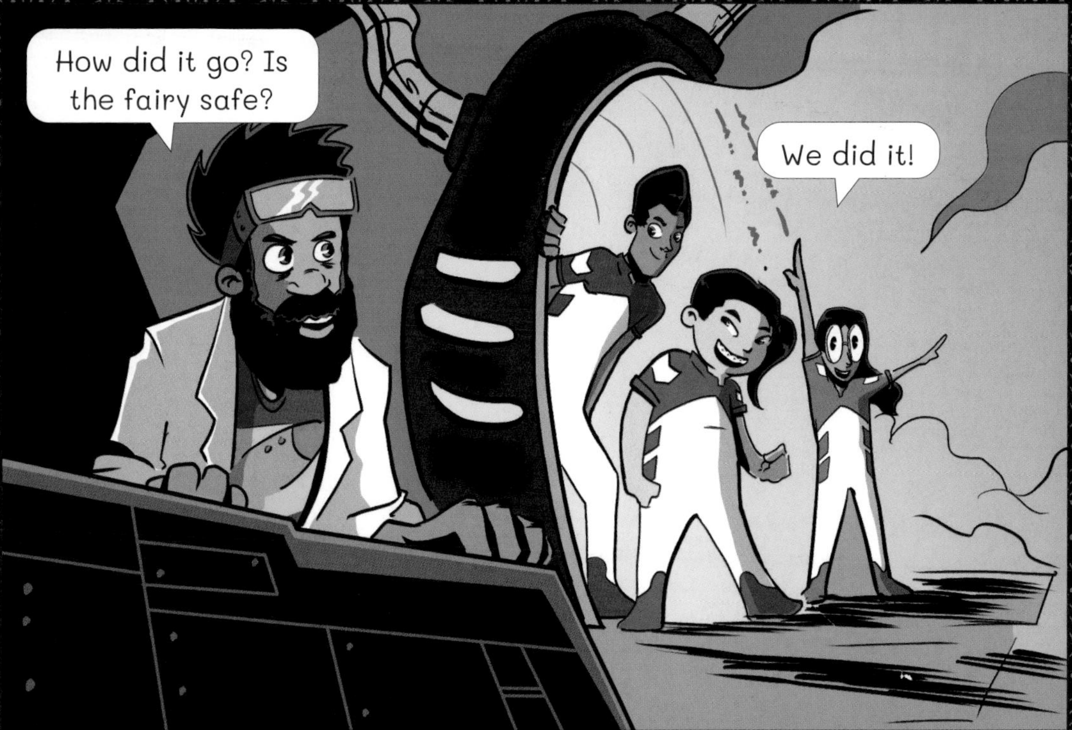
How did it go? Is the fairy safe?
We did it!

Every morning, every evening, ain't we got fun...
YEAH!
YAY!
GO GIRL!
WOO!

SURVIVAL TIPS

You need to be careful around fairies. They are very clever. Here are some important tips to stay safe.

* Never say you don't believe in them. A fairy will die. And other fairies will punish you.

* Never brag that you can **outwit** a fairy. You will offend the fairy. They will try to prove you wrong.

* Never drink or eat anything from the fairy world. You'll be stuck there.

* Be kind and moral. Fairies dislike people who are greedy, mean, and lazy.

* If people have put buildings and roads over ancient fairy homes, do not go to these places. Fairies will be angry.

* Know the names of fairies. Calling a fairy by name gives you control. But be careful, because telling them your name gives them control over you.

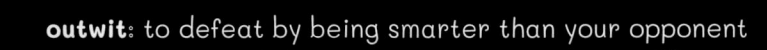

outwit: to defeat by being smarter than your opponent

BECOME A SONGWRITER

Some of the greatest songwriters in the modern world wrote during the 1920s. Duke Ellington was famous for his jazz songs. His music, such as "It Don't Mean a Thing (If It Ain't Got That Swing)," is still played today.

Writing song lyrics is a great way to tell a story or share your feelings. You can practice with music you already know.

* Pick a popular song you like.

* Use a computer to look up the lyrics. What does the rhyme look like? Does the song use rhyming words at the end of each line? Does it create a pattern? Some common lyric patterns are:
  AA, BB, CC, etc.
  This means that the words at the end of the first line and the second line rhyme. Then a different rhyme is used for the third and fourth line, and so on.
  or
  ABAC, DEDF, etc.
  This means that the first line and the third line rhyme, but the second and fourth do not.

You can decide what works best for your song.

* Replace the words with your own. Tell your own story.

* Ask a parent to help you record your new lyrics to the music you chose.

What worked in your process? What was the hardest part? What did you like the most? Share your song with friends and keep trying new ways to tell stories.

LEARN MORE

BOOKS

Pinkney, Andrea. *Duke Ellington.* New York, NY: Hyperion Book for Children, 2007.

Myers, Walter Dean. *Jazz.* New York, NY: Holiday House, 2008.

Ringgold, Faith. *Harlem Renaissance Party.* New York, NY: HarperCollins, 2015.

WEBSITES

Ducksters—US History: The Roaring Twenties
https://www.ducksters.com/history/us_1900s/roaring_twenties.php

KidsKonnect—The Harlem Renaissance
https://kidskonnect.com/social-studies/harlem-renaissance

THE MONSTER HUNTER TEAM

JORGE
TÍO HECTOR'S NEPHEW, JORGE, LOVES MUSIC. AT 16 HE IS ONE OF THE OLDEST MONSTER HUNTERS AND LEADER OF THE GROUP.

MARCUS
MARCUS IS 14 AND IS WISE BEYOND HIS YEARS. HE IS A PROBLEM SOLVER, OFTEN GETTING THE GROUP OUT OF STICKY SITUATIONS.

FIONA
FIONA IS FIERCE AND PROTECTIVE. AT 16 SHE IS A ROLLER DERBY CHAMPION AND IS ONE OF JORGE'S CLOSEST FRIENDS.

ELENA
ELENA IS JORGE'S LITTLE SISTER AND TÍO HECTOR'S NIECE. AT 14, SHE IS THE HEART AND SOUL OF THE GROUP. ELENA IS KIND, THOUGHTFUL, AND SINCERE.

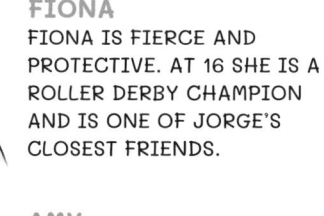

AMY
AMY IS 15. SHE LOVES BOOKS AND HISTORY. AMY AND ELENA SPEND ALMOST EVERY WEEKEND TOGETHER. THEY ARE ATTACHED AT THE HIP.

TÍO HECTOR
JORGE AND ELENA'S TÍO IS THE MASTERMIND BEHIND THE MONSTER HUNTERS. HIS TIME TRAVEL MACHINE MAKES IT ALL POSSIBLE.

GLOSSARY

ancient (AYN-chent) being very, very old

chanteuse (shan-TOOZ) a female singer, especially one who sings in nightclubs

duet (doo-ET) a piece of music sung by two people

economy (ee-KAH-nuh-mee) the system of making and using money in a particular location.

Great Depression (GRAYT deh-PREH-shun) a financial slump in the United States that started in 1929.

outwit (owt-WIT) to defeat by being smarter than your opponent

realm (RELM) a kingdom or land

reliable (ree-LAI-uh-bul) able to be trusted

renaissance (REN-uh-sahns) a rebirth of art and culture

rowhouses (ROH-how-zez) rows of houses that share side walls

sacred (SAY-kred) respected by a particular group or individual

tío (TEE-oh) "uncle" in Spanish

VIP (VEE-AI-PEE) stands for "very important person"

wily (WAI-lee) good at gaining advantage over others

INDEX